Angelina Ballerina

My First Ballet Class

This book belongs to

Written by **Katharine** Holabird
With illustrations by **Helen** Craig

LONDON, NEW YORK, MUNICH,
MELBOURNE, AND DELHI

Project Editor Lindsay Fernandes
Designer Lynne Moulding
Senior Designer Lisa Lanzarini
Publishing Manager Cynthia O'Neill Collins
Art Director Mark Richards
Category Publisher Alex Kirkham
Production Rochelle Talary
DTP Dean Scholey

First published in Great Britain in 2005 by Dorling Kindersley Limited,
80 Strand, London WC2R 0RL
A Penguin Company

05 06 07 08 09 10 9 8 7 6 5 4 3 2 1

A CIP catalogue record for this book is available from the British Library.

ISBN 1-4053-0851-6

Reproduced by Media, Development and Printing, Ltd., UK
Printed and bound at L.E.G.O., Italy

Discover more at
www.dk.com

Contents

I love to dance!

If you enjoy dancing then you'll love going to ballet classes. You'll learn lots of ballet steps and enjoy practising them with your friends. Ballet class is so much fun – it's the best thing since cheddar cheese!

I just can't stop dancing!

Before you go

It's so exciting when you start ballet lessons. Every day you've been thinking about ballet, and looking forward to dancing in your ballet slippers and leotard, and now the big day has finally arrived. You can't wait to put on your ballet clothes, point your toes, and dance!

I even dance in my dreams!

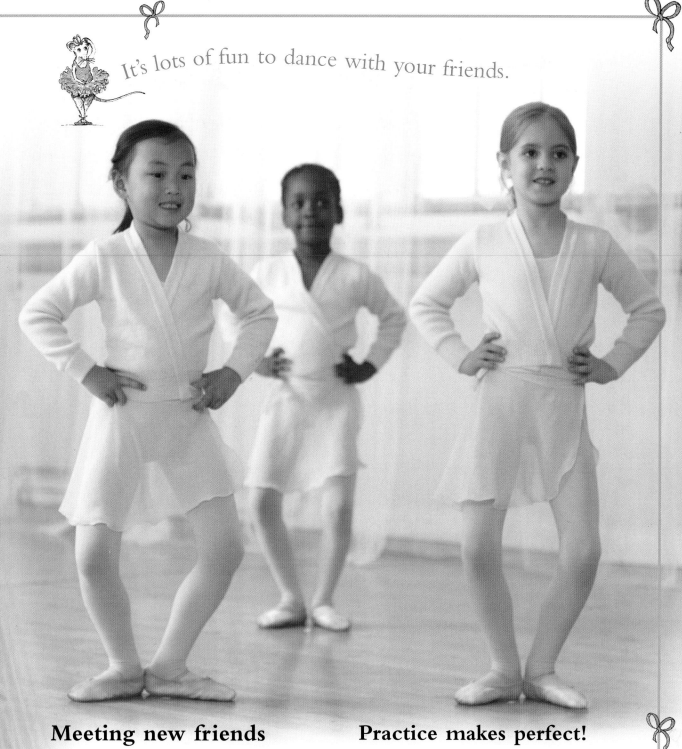

It's lots of fun to dance with your friends.

Meeting new friends

When you go to ballet class you'll meet lots of other young dancers. You can practise all the ballet positions together, and soon you won't feel shy at all!

Practice makes perfect!

At first the ballet positions may seem a bit strange, but don't worry. Your teacher will encourage you, and show you how to get the positions right.

What to wear

I love to go to ballet lessons – they're so much fun! I pack all the things I will need in my ballet bag. You don't have to bring much, just some ballet slippers to dance in and comfortable clothes to move around in.

I put all my ballet things in a special bag.

Ready to dance
You'll need a stretchy leotard with a pair of tights and a swirly skirt. Don't forget your ballet slippers!

Pretty in pink
My favourite colour is pink, but there are lots of other pretty colours you can choose from.

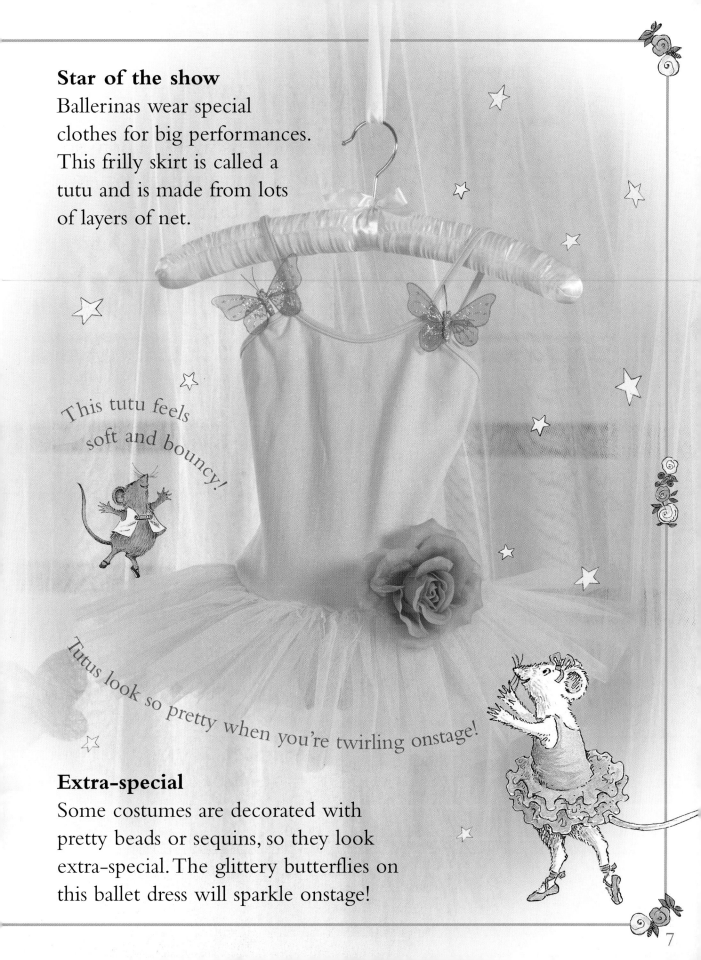

Star of the show

Ballerinas wear special
clothes for big performances.
This frilly skirt is called a
tutu and is made from lots
of layers of net.

This tutu feels soft and bouncy!

Tutus look so pretty when you're twirling onstage!

Extra-special

Some costumes are decorated with
pretty beads or sequins, so they look
extra-special. The glittery butterflies on
this ballet dress will sparkle onstage!

Ready for class

The first thing you do when you arrive at ballet school is get changed. As soon as you put on your leotard, tights, and slippers you'll be ready to start. It's a good idea to bring a hairbrush and some pretty hairbands so you can fix your hair.

Ballet friends help each other.

Ballet slippers

There are special ballet shops where you can buy your ballet slippers. When you try on a pair of slippers make sure they are comfortable and you have room to wiggle your toes!

Looking neat

Dancers need to be neat and tidy. They tie back their hair so they can see properly. If you can't tie your own ribbons, ask a classmate to help.

Ballerinas always tie their ribbons carefully so they won't trip over.

I wear a pretty ribbon in my hair.

Pointe shoes

Grown-up ballerinas have to look neat and tidy too. They wear ballet slippers called 'pointe' shoes that are fastened with ribbons around their ankles. The ribbons are tied in a special way so that they look neat and won't come undone.

Lesson time!

Ballet lessons take place in a big room called a studio, where there is lots of space for dancing. There are mirrors on the walls so you can check your ballet positions, and a smooth wooden floor to dance on.

Miss Lilly is the best ballet teacher in all of Mouseland!

Music

In class you'll dance to lots of different types of music, sometimes fast and sometimes slow. There may be a pianist or you might dance to music from a tape or CD player.

Miss Quaver plays the piano in my ballet classes!

Stand in line!

At the start of every ballet lesson the children line up in front of the teacher while she takes the register. This is so she can check who is present. It's hard to wait patiently – but as soon as your name is ticked you'll be ready to dance.

The teacher is pleased to see all the children.

Warming up

Mouselings always warm up their tails!

At the start of each class you should always warm up your muscles so you are ready to dance. Here are some fun stretching exercises to help you warm up. Remember to go slowly and really s-t-r-e-t-c-h!

Pitter-patter

Sit on the floor with your legs crossed. To warm up your hands pretend it's raining and use your fingers to show raindrops falling down from the sky.

A growing seed

To warm up your arms pretend you are a tiny seed that has been planted in the earth. Slowly lift your arms up in the air. As you stretch your arms way up high, imagine you are growing into a tall tree.

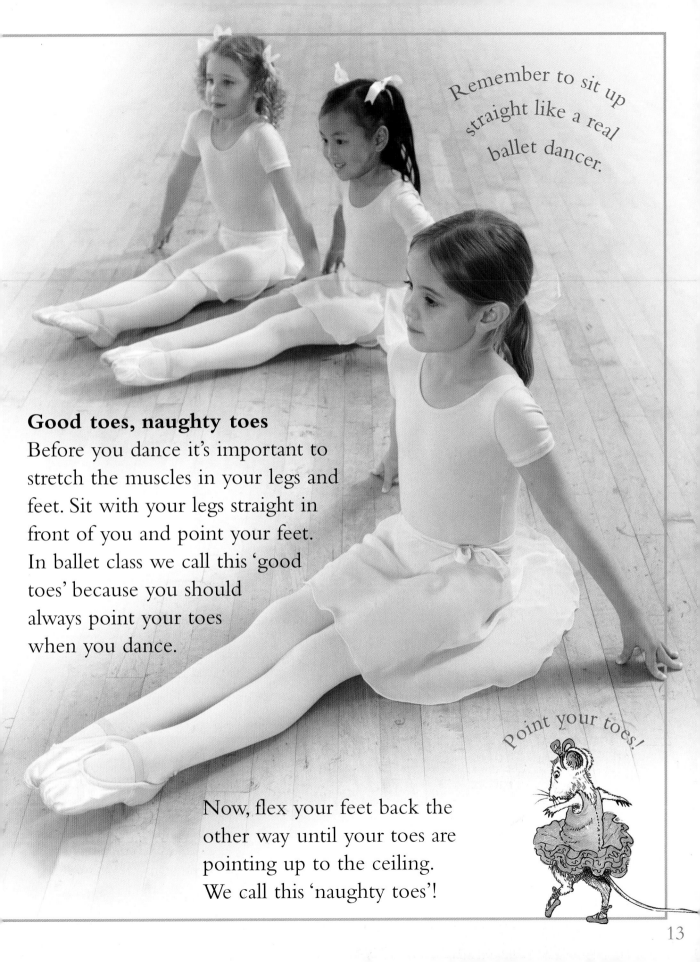

Remember to sit up straight like a real ballet dancer.

Good toes, naughty toes

Before you dance it's important to stretch the muscles in your legs and feet. Sit with your legs straight in front of you and point your feet. In ballet class we call this 'good toes' because you should always point your toes when you dance.

Now, flex your feet back the other way until your toes are pointing up to the ceiling. We call this 'naughty toes'!

Point your toes!

Dancing together

One of the best things about going to ballet classes is dancing with your new friends. There are all kinds of fun steps you can try but it can take a little while to get used to dancing with a partner or in a group.

Working together
In groups of three the dancers listen to everyone's ideas before they decide on their dance routine.

I'm a little dancing seed!

Dancing flowers
They decide to be dancing flowers and pretend to grow from little seeds into big beautiful flowers.

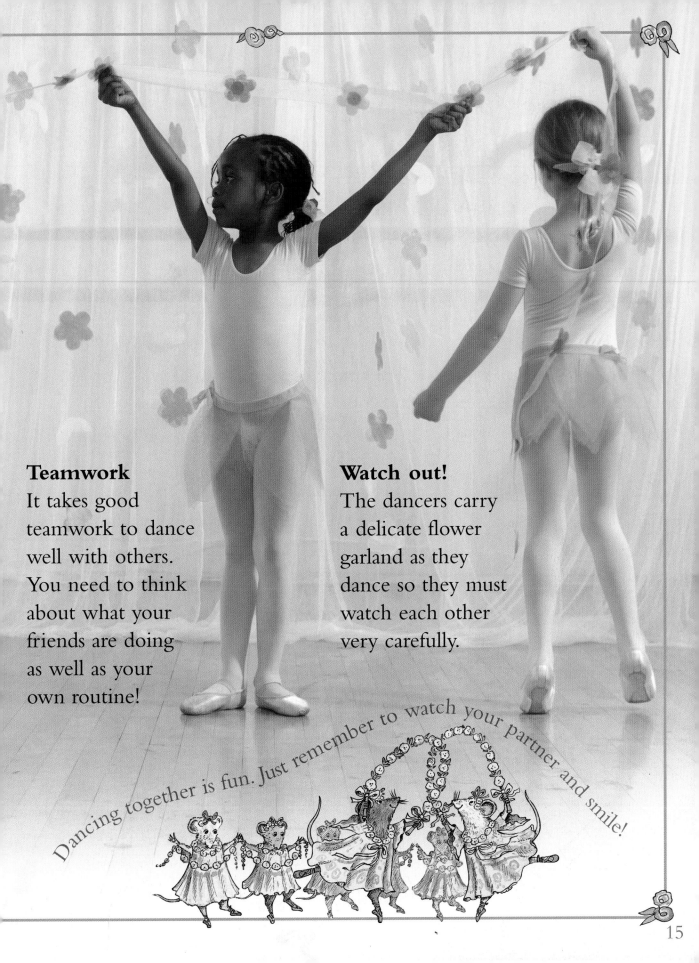

Teamwork
It takes good teamwork to dance well with others. You need to think about what your friends are doing as well as your own routine!

Watch out!
The dancers carry a delicate flower garland as they dance so they must watch each other very carefully.

Dancing together is fun. Just remember to watch your partner and smile!

Jump up high!

I love to watch ballet dancers doing lots of exciting jumps and leaps – they look like they're as light as feathers! At ballet class you will learn some simple jumps at first, and with practice you'll soon be jumping for joy!

Jumping is lots of fun!

Jack-in-the-box
Pretend you are a jack-in-the-box ready to pop up. Be still and don't wiggle!

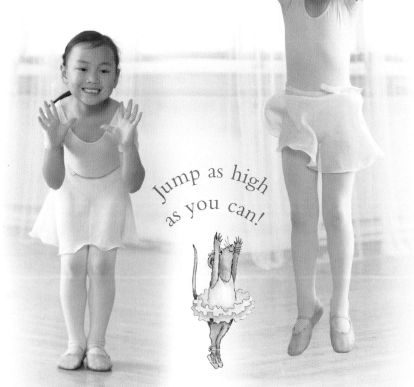

Jump as high as you can!

1. Start with your knees bent and your hands on the floor in front of you. Get ready to jump...

2. Imagine someone has taken the lid off the box. Push down into the floor as you spring up.

3. Jump way up with your back straight and your arms stretched up high. Remember to point your toes.

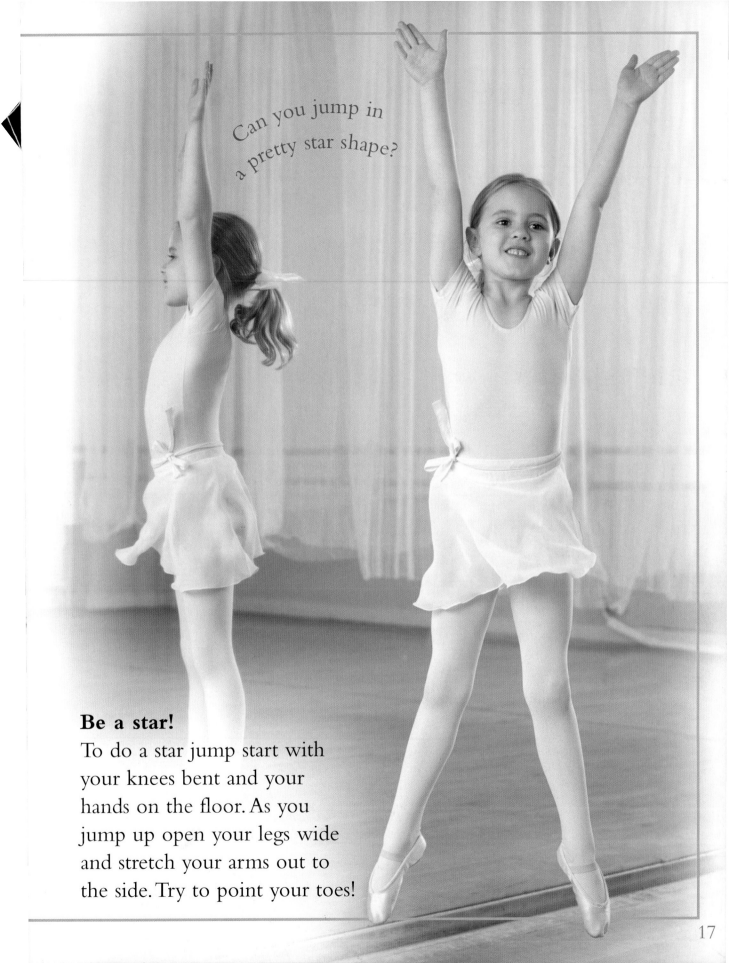

Can you jump in a pretty star shape?

Be a star!

To do a star jump start with your knees bent and your hands on the floor. As you jump up open your legs wide and stretch your arms out to the side. Try to point your toes!

Dressing up

Wearing a costume when you dance is lots of fun and can really help you to get into character! In today's class the little dancers are all dressed up in special outfits. Can you guess what they are?

Be a butterfly
The children are pretending to be beautiful butterflies! They wear colourful tutus and sparkly wings. When they dance they imagine they are flying around a lovely garden.

It's fun to dress up!

Listen to the music and soon you'll be flying!

Let's pretend
Gently raise and lower your arms in graceful movements and you'll feel just like a butterfly fluttering its wings.

Be delicate
Take little steps in time to the music, and be as delicate as a butterfly as you dance.

Telling a story

Ballet is a way of telling a story using dance instead of words. Ballet dancers use their faces and bodies when they perform so the audience understands what is happening in the story even though there are no words. It's magic!

I love to dress up and practise making faces!

In the mirror

Try using your face and body to tell a story. Practise making faces like these and see if your classmates can guess what you're trying to show.

Surprised
To show you are surprised, put your hands on your face and open your mouth wide!

Sad
To pretend you are sad, tilt your head down and look towards the ground.

Happy
Showing that you are happy is really easy! All you have to do is smile!

Love

To show 'love' put both your hands upon your heart and look up. Try thinking about all the people you care about.

Sleep

To pretend you are sleepy, close your eyes and rest your head on your arms as if you are lying on a lovely soft pillow.

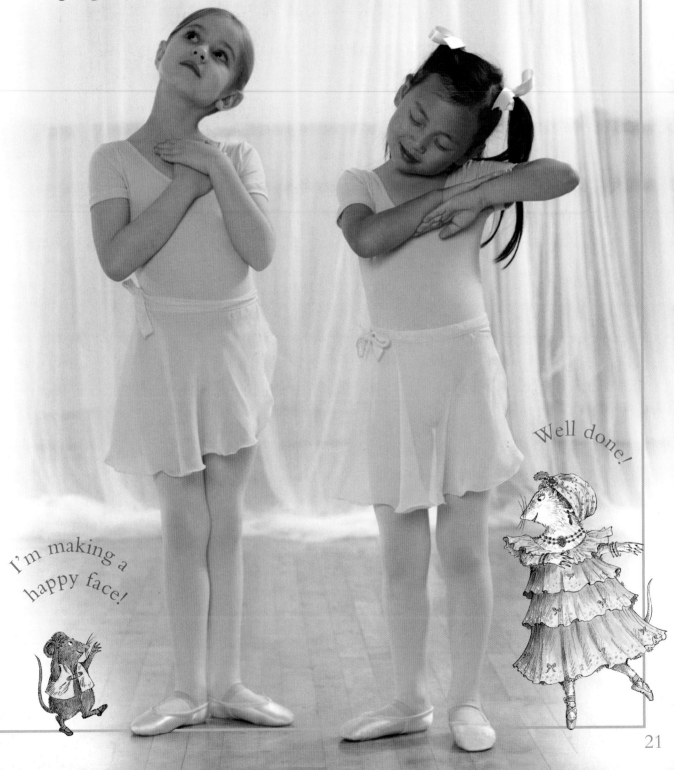

I'm making a happy face!

Well done!

Famous ballets

Many wonderful stories have been transformed into exciting ballets. Some ballets like *Sleeping Beauty* and *Cinderella* are based on fairy tales that you probably know very well! Here are just a few of the famous ballets performed onstage all around the world.

Swan Lake
A beautiful princess called Odette is turned into a white swan by an evil wizard. A prince falls in love with her and tries to save her.

Sleeping Beauty
Princess Aurora pricks her finger on a spinning wheel and falls asleep under a magic spell. To wake up she must be kissed by her true love.

What's your favourite ballet?

Cinderella
Cinderella's step-sisters won't let her go to the ball. Just when all hope is lost, her Fairy Godmother appears and makes her the belle of the ball!

Coppelia
Coppelia is a doll who looks so real that people think she's alive! Everyone falls in love with her, even the old toymaker!

23

Henry loves to make up his own dances.

Imagine!

When you dance you can be anything you want to be – all you have to do is use your imagination. Sometimes during class, the teacher lets you create your own special dances.

Listen to the music

The music that's playing helps the class create their dance. As they listen to the music they think about whether it is fast or slow, happy or sad. How does the music make them feel?

Galloping

The music reminds the class of the sound of horses' hooves and they decide to dance like little ponies. They trot across the room in time to the music.

Clip-clop, clip-clop!

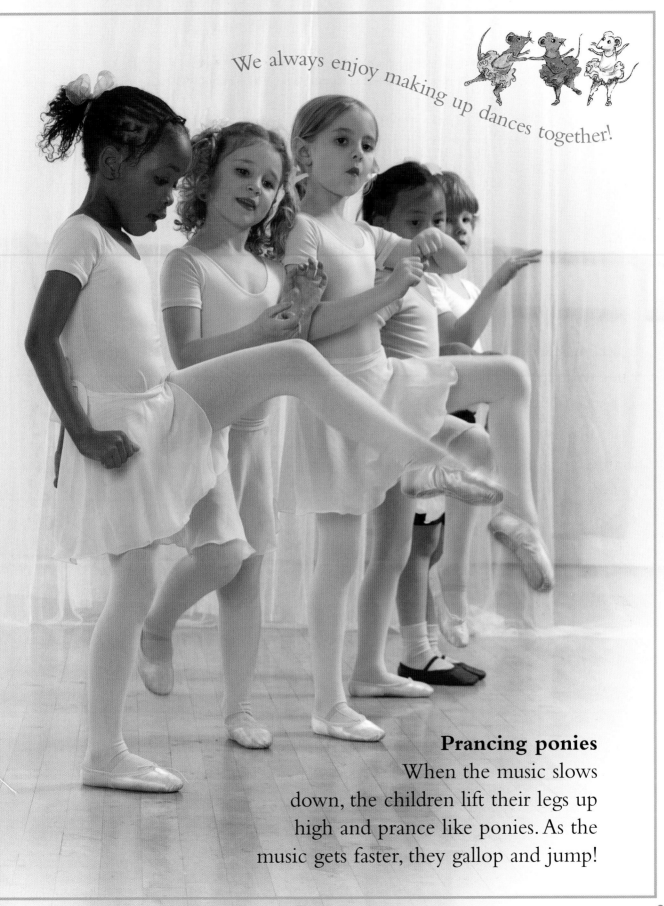

We always enjoy making up dances together!

Prancing ponies
When the music slows down, the children lift their legs up high and prance like ponies. As the music gets faster, they gallop and jump!

Ballerina dreams

Sometimes a real ballerina comes to class to tell you all about being a dancer. It's exciting – especially if she brings a beautiful costume! This ballerina has been dancing for years but once upon a time she was a beginner too!

This is my best costume!

Costumes

Ballet costumes are so pretty and sparkly. Each costume is specially made by hand to fit the ballerina perfectly.

Decorations

This costume is decorated with lots of sequins and beads.

This is the prettiest tutu ever!

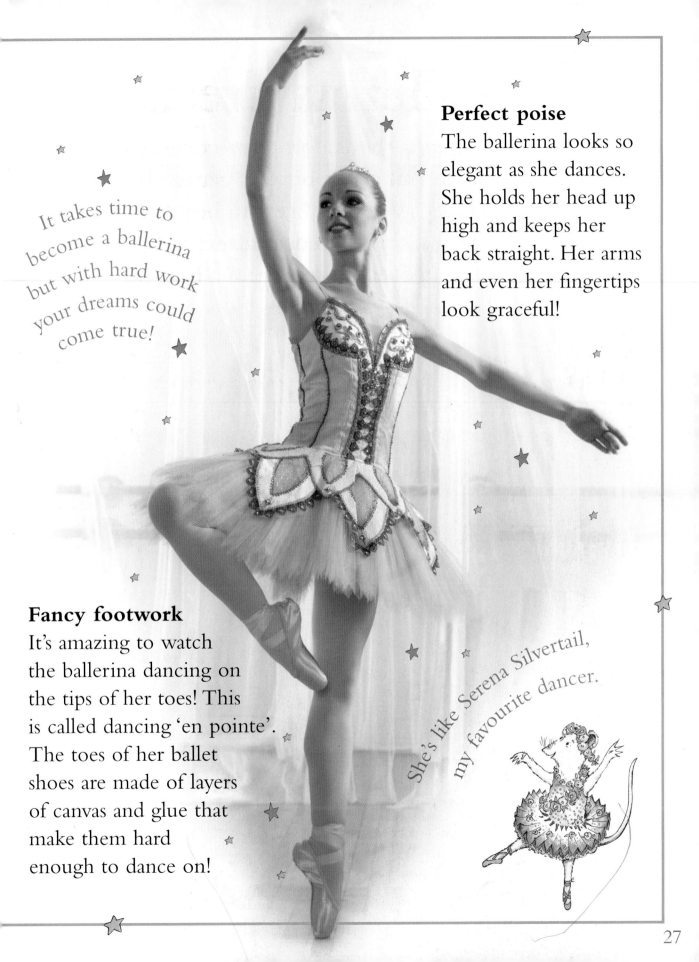

It takes time to become a ballerina but with hard work your dreams could come true!

Perfect poise

The ballerina looks so elegant as she dances. She holds her head up high and keeps her back straight. Her arms and even her fingertips look graceful!

Fancy footwork

It's amazing to watch the ballerina dancing on the tips of her toes! This is called dancing 'en pointe'. The toes of her ballet shoes are made of layers of canvas and glue that make them hard enough to dance on!

She's like Serena Silvertail, my favourite dancer.

Show time!

At the end of term many ballet schools put on a performance. It's a chance for young dancers to show people what they have learnt. A performance takes lots of preparation and hard work but it's exciting and lots of fun too!

Miss Lilly helps us prepare for our shows.

Dress rehearsals

A few days before the show you have a dress rehearsal. This is when you all get dressed up in your costumes and practise your dance.

Practice makes perfect!

Make-up

Make-up helps the audience to see your face as you dance. The dress rehearsal is the time to try out your make-up before the real show.

Get into character

You can also use make-up to create characters. You could be an animal, a clown, or even a wicked witch! With your make-up done and your costume on you'll feel transformed!

What are these dancers going to be?

Here we go!

After the finishing touches are done it's time to practise your routine one last time before the big day!

Don't be late for rehearsals, Henry!

A mouse ballet

When it's time for the show to begin, the
music plays and the dancers wait behind
the curtain. They are a little nervous at
first but they quickly begin to enjoy
themselves. The dancers are being happy
little mice – just like me and my friends!

Ready to go
The dancers have
made mouse ears
and tails! They even
have whiskers and
tiny noses like us!

Coming onstage
One by one the
dancers tiptoe
onstage as quiet
as little mice!

On with the show!

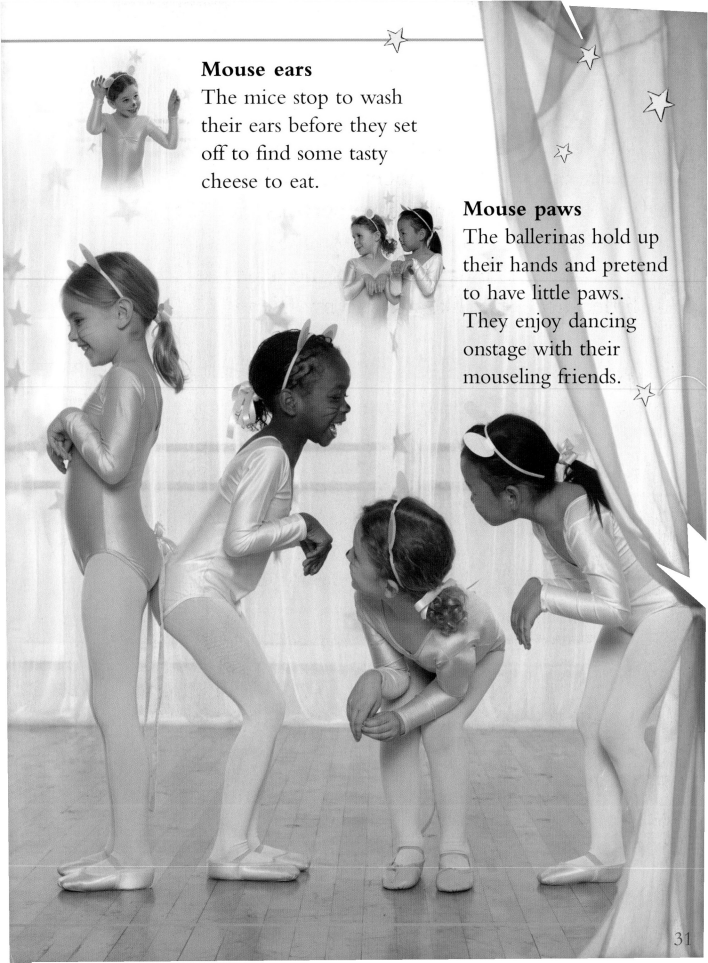

Mouse ears

The mice stop to wash their ears before they set off to find some tasty cheese to eat.

Mouse paws

The ballerinas hold up their hands and pretend to have little paws. They enjoy dancing onstage with their mouseling friends.

See you next time!

Acknowledgements

Dorling Kindersley would to thank the following for their help in preparing and producing this book:

All the pupils of Central School of Ballet who attended the photo shoot; Central School of Ballet for their kind permission to photograph the book there; Maggie Purr who trained and graduated from Central School of Ballet and now teaches there, for her time, advice and patience during the photo shoot; Daisy Jackson and Katie Price at HIT Entertainment for all their help.